The
New Baby
at Your House

The
New Baby
at Your House

JOANNA COLE

photographs by
Hella Hammid

William Morrow and Company, Inc.

New York

The author would like to thank Louise Bates Ames, Co-director of the Gesell Institute for Human Development, and Daisy Edmondson, former Senior Editor of *Parents* magazine, for reading and suggesting changes in the manuscript for this book. Thanks also to Margo Rideout for asking for a book that tells *all* sides to having a new sibling.

A Note To Parents

When a new baby is born in a family, it is natural for an older sibling to have all kinds of feelings. One child may be proud of being a big sister. Another may be worried that he will be displaced by the newcomer. Yet another may seem too busy with her own life to have much interest in the new baby. Whatever a child's dominant feeling, however, it is likely that others are there, too. A child may have negative feelings or worries that he tries to keep hidden. Or he may feel different things at different times: loving one moment, competitive the next, angry at his parents for the whole situation.

A parent's job is not to "fix things" so the negative feelings will go away and everyone will be happy all the time. Children don't need to be protected from the realization that their parents can love and care for another child. But they do need time to adjust to a new situation. And they need to have their feelings acknowledged and to feel included in the family.

The first way to include the older child or children in the family is to *prepare* them for the arrival of the new baby. Keeping a first child in the dark about the expected baby is unfair. Children under three probably shouldn't be told right away because their sense of time is so limited that they can't comprehend an event that will take place eight months hence. Nevertheless, it is important to tell a small child about the baby by the time the pregnancy shows, before he learns it from others. If a child senses that a secret is being kept from him, he begins the relationship to his sibling with a feeling of being left out.

It is also considerate to include older children in some of the activities during the pregnancy. For instance, they can come along on a visit to the obstetrician and hear the baby's heartbeat.

In preparing for the arrival, it is helpful to talk about the baby. But it is not advisable to make false promises, such as "The baby will be someone for you to play with." Such a promise is bound to end up disappointing an older sibling, because, at first, the baby will do little else but eat, cry, and sleep. The best course is to be truthful and realistic about what it is like to have a baby in the house. One way to do this is to read this book with your child and to visit some families that have newborns.

Sometimes a child may withdraw or simply may not want to talk about the baby. If this happens, don't force your child to talk about it, and don't tell him how you think he "really" feels. But do let him know you are available, saying, "I'll be glad to answer any questions you may have about the baby" or "Some children have worries when a new baby is coming. If you have any, you can tell me about them." Often young children "talk about" their feelings in play, rather than words. Ordinary play can help a child express himself, especially if you provide a family of dolls that includes parents, an older child, and a baby.

Most childcare experts advise against scheduling a lot of changes immediately before or after the birth, especially for toddlers and young children. Adjusting to the baby will be change enough. If you can help it, avoid such transitions as starting nursery school, hiring a new sitter, graduating from a crib to a bed, or learning to use the toilet. These events should happen well before the baby is due or be postponed until later.

As the birth approaches, a child needs to know exactly what will happen when the baby is born. Although some babies will be born at home, the vast majority of children will be separated from their mother for a few days while she is at a hospital or childbirth center. In this case, the child needs to be told that you will be away for a few days, where you will be, and what arrangements have been made for him. Experts say that it's usually best for the older child to stay at home in familiar surroundings with people who have cared for him before. The ideal arrangement may be for the father to take time off from work and stay with the child.

Separation from you is difficult, and the younger the child, the more difficult it will be. Experts urge parents to say good-bye to their children before they leave for the hospital, even if it means waking them up to do so. They may cry, but they will

6

feel more secure if they know what is happening and do not wake up to find you gone.

Contact with you while you are away is essential. Studies have shown that children who are able to visit their mothers in the hospital make a better adjustment to the new baby than others, even if they appear very upset at parting. If the hospital resists the idea of a visit, perhaps your doctor or midwife can intercede for you.

Even if your child is not able to visit, frequent phone conversations will ease the separation. Talk about the baby a bit, but remember that your first child is more interested in *you* than the baby, and he needs attention from you. So most of the conversation should be about what is happening at home and acknowledgment that he misses you, and that you miss him.

Many families report that older siblings benefit from coming along when mother and baby leave the hospital, even if children are required to stay in the reception area with a friend or relative. The fact that you want your child there and spend time paying attention to her will reassure her about her importance to you.

Once at home, follow your child's lead as to whether she wants to look at the baby or just spend time with you. At some point, however, encourage her to inspect the baby and to help with feeding, bathing, and changing. Let her touch and hold the baby while sitting safely in an armchair.

With toddlers, feelings will change from positive to negative very quickly, and young children are more likely to express these feelings through actions than words. Therefore, toddlers should never be left alone with a baby. Stay close and be prepared to intercept any inappropriate moves physically.

Teach your child in a positive way that gentleness is the rule with babies. Avoid the words "don't" and "no" as much as possible. Instead, say encouraging things like "Be gentle, that's right" and "I like the way you hold her so carefully."

An older sibling is usually delighted when the baby responds to her in any way, such as watching her face, squeezing a finger, turning the head in response to a stroke on the cheek. When parents make a point of mentioning this responsiveness, it seems to help a child develop a loving feeling for the baby. One mother told me, "I always said to Christopher, 'Brian loves you' and 'He is happy when you talk to him.' Now that Brian is almost two, they get along very well most of the time."

When the baby becomes mobile, older siblings often feel their territory is being invaded. Children are not really able to work out problems like these on their own. They need help from their parents to find ways of protecting their toys and space. At other times, parents can show children how to include the baby in games. And they can be most helpful by explaining babies' behavior—for instance, babies grab toys because they are curious, babies want to be near big sisters and brothers because they love them—and by showing that babies can easily be distracted if they are offered a different toy or activity.

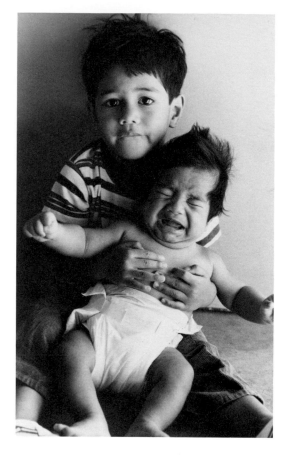

From the time they first find out about the baby until they must cope with a tag-along toddler, older brothers and sisters have several needs. They need regular time alone with both mother and father, time when they are the center of attention and love. They need help from parents to control their aggressive impulses toward the younger child. They need a chance to express sad, angry, or jealous feelings (not to be confused with aggressive *actions*). And they need to have their parents accept these feelings without trying to explain them away.

Most of all, children need to be reassured through words and actions that the arrival of the baby does not mean they have been replaced. Show your child that he can be loved and attended to in the presence of the baby. That he can be included in caring for and playing with the baby. And that he will always be an important, unique person in the family, no matter how large it may be.

FURTHER READING FOR PARENTS

He Hit Me First: When Brothers and Sisters Fight by Louise Bates Ames and others. New York: Dembner Books, 1982. A realistic book about sibling rivalry by the well-known authority on child development. The book contains an especially good chapter on the arrival of a new baby, as well as a discussion of how much sibling rivalry is to be expected and how to cope with daily life in the family.

Raising Siblings by Carole and Andrew Calladine. New York: Delacorte Press, 1979. The authors are family counselors and parents of four sons, two of whom are adopted. Their book offers original and imaginative solutions to everyday sibling conflicts. Especially helpful are their explanation of why treating all children the *same* isn't necessarily *fair* and their description of how responding to each child's special needs instead can ease rivalry.

Welcoming Your Second Baby by Vicki Lansky. New York: Bantam, 1984. Part of the author's "Practical Parenting" series, this fast-reading book combines basic advice with quotes from parents who've "been there." It's hard to think of any issue about the new baby that isn't covered here with brevity and wisdom.

Your Second Child: A Guide for Parents by Joan Solomon Weiss. New York: Summit Books, 1981. A well-researched look at the decision to have a second child, the effect of birth-order on a child's personality, and recommended ways of handling sibling rivalry.

Is there a new baby at your house?

When Jeffrey's mother was pregnant, her belly got very big. That is because the baby was inside her body, in a special place called her womb, or uterus. Jeffrey could feel the baby moving and kicking.

12

Susan's mother was pregnant, too. Susan liked to pretend that the baby could understand her when she talked. She would ask the baby all kinds of questions, such as, "Are you warm in there?" or "Would you like some cornflakes?"

When a baby is about to be born, most mothers go to the hospital. When Ashley's mother went away, she missed her very much. It helped to talk with her on the phone.

Daniel visited the hospital. He hugged
his mother and got his first look at Andrea,
his new baby sister.

When it was time for Ashley's mother to come home, she went with her father to the hospital to pick her up. Ashley was glad to see her mother.

She helped her mother with the suitcase and sat with her in the car.

At home, Davis wanted to look at his
baby sister, Shelly. He was amazed at how
little she was.

"Look at her tiny toes!" he said.

Shelly was a sleepy baby. When she woke
up, she stayed awake for only a little while.
Then her eyes closed and she was asleep
again.

Davis noticed that a piece of the umbilical cord was still attached to Shelly's belly. All new babies have this. After a while, the cord will dry up and fall off. Only a little scab will be left. When the scab heals, it will leave a navel, or belly button, just like yours.

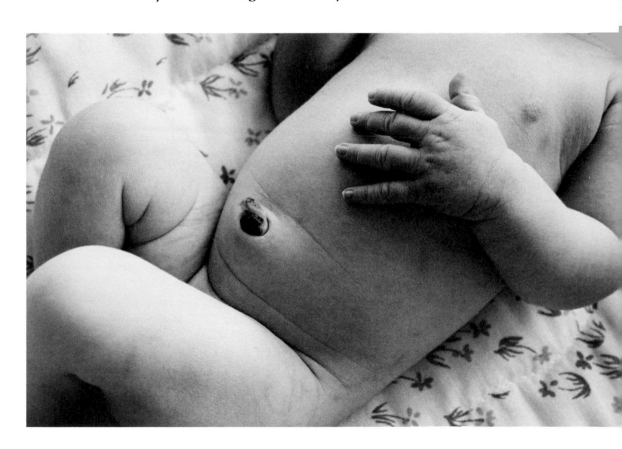

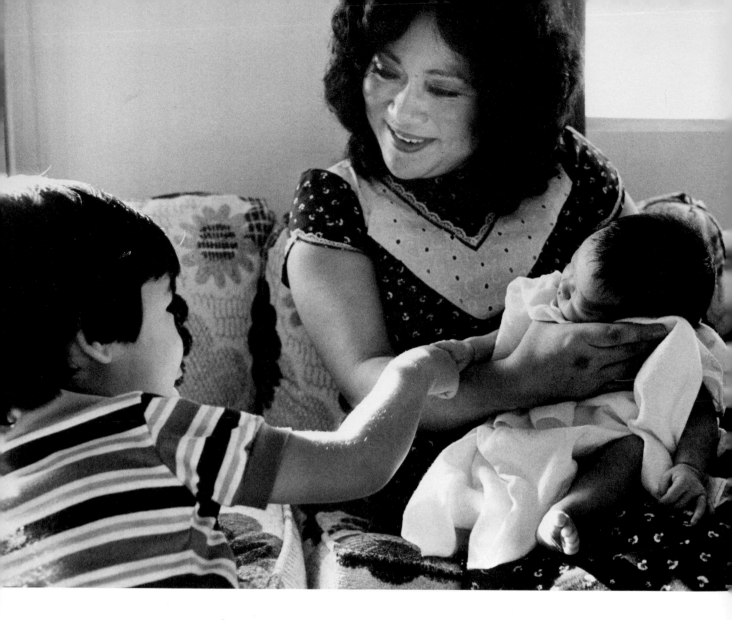

Newborn babies are not very strong.
They cannot even lift their heads up.
   Davis's mother helped him learn to be
gentle with his baby sister.

New babies are small and need to be taken care of. But even so, they can do many things. Right after they are born, babies can see, hear, taste, smell, feel, and cry. (Did you know that at first babies don't shed tears when they cry? These will come later.)

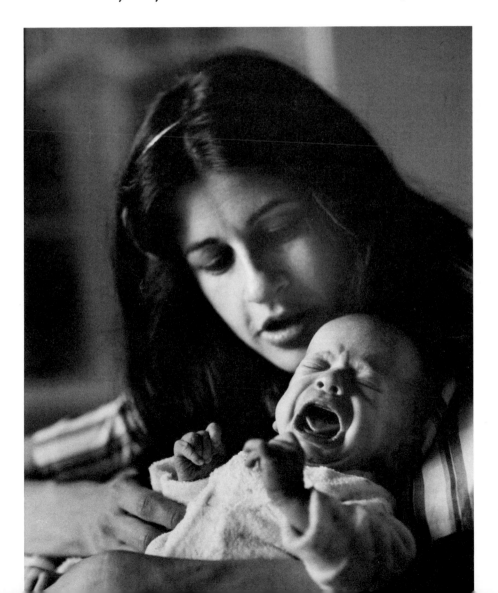

Babies are born knowing how to suck. They don't have any teeth, so they can't eat solid food. Instead, they suck milk from their mother's breast or from a bottle.

When Jocelyn gently stroked Michael's cheek, he turned his head toward her hand, and he made sucking motions. Jocelyn put her finger in his mouth. It tickled when the baby sucked her finger.

Your parents can help you try this with your baby, too. But don't forget to wash your hands first.

Very young babies can also grip very
tight. Davis's baby sister squeezed his finger
so hard her tiny fingers turned white.
    You can get your baby to grip your finger
by gently stroking the baby's palm.

Babies like to look at faces and bright colors. Jocelyn's brother, Michael, likes to watch her talk. Sometimes Jocelyn moves a toy back and forth in front of the baby. Michael's eyes follow the toy.

You can try this, too. If your brother or sister looks away, it means the baby is tired of looking and needs a rest.

Big brothers and sisters have a lot of feelings about babies.

Diana felt proud to be a big sister. She told her friends at school about baby Christopher.

She felt very grown-up when she helped
her father change the baby's diaper.

But when Christopher cried, Diana got
upset. She put her fingers in her ears. "Can't
you make him stop?" she asked her mother.

Diana's mother explained that babies have
to cry. That is how they tell people they
need something. Diana understood, but
she still didn't like it when the baby cried.

Davis felt left out when the guests all wanted to see the baby. No one seemed to ask about him.

Davis wished he could be a baby, too. Then he would get all the attention.

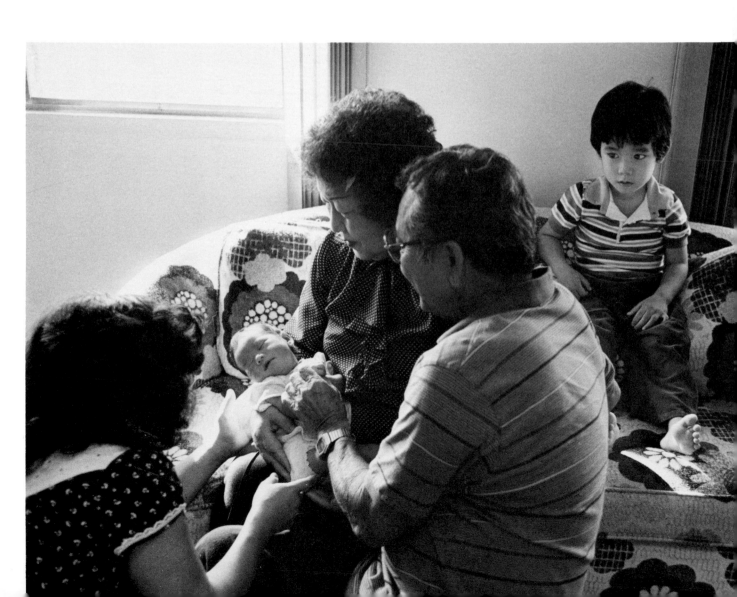

Jason wanted his mother to play with him "right now." He was angry because he had to wait until after the baby's bath.

"I don't want a baby sister anymore," Jason said. "Take her back!"

Once Jason got so angry that he wanted to hit the baby. But his mommy wouldn't let him. "It's okay to be mad," said Mommy, "but I can't let you hurt the baby."

Diana worried that her mommy and
daddy didn't love her anymore. "All you
care about is the baby," she said.

Mommy told her they would *never* stop
loving her. "You are very special to us," she
said. Then Mommy and Daddy held Diana
in their arms and hugged her tight.

Sometimes David wished he could be the only child again. He liked it when the baby was sleeping, and he could have special time alone with his mommy. He felt happy and excited when his daddy took him to the zoo all by himself.

Do you ever have feelings like these? It's okay to have a lot of *different* feelings when a baby is born in your family.

Noah said his feelings about the baby were "all mixed up." Sometimes he liked his baby sister. At other times, he got mad at Lucy when his parents made him pick up his toys. Lucy never had to do any chores.

Often Noah wished his parents would baby *him*. But he also wanted to be treated like a big boy.

It's fun being big. Older sisters and brothers can do a lot of things babies can't do.

A baby needs to be changed. Big brothers and sisters learn to use the toilet. Baby Michael sucks on a bottle. But his big sister, Jocelyn, eats pizza.

Babies sleep in cribs. Older children have big beds.

Jeffrey has lots of friends. But his baby sister is too small to have any.

Now that Diana is a big girl, she doesn't need to be fed and changed like a baby. But Mommy and Daddy still take care of her in other ways. They help her learn new things, they hold her hand when she is scared, they sing her favorite bedtime songs, and they listen when she talks about her ideas.

When Emily was six years old, her sister Allison was only three. Now Allison is six years old, but Emily is nine. Emily will always be older than Allison.

Your baby brother or sister will grow up, too. But you will always be the older one, and your little sister or brother will always be the younger one. Even when you are both teenagers. Even when you are both grown-ups!

As babies grow, they get bigger, taller, and heavier. They get more hair. And teeth start coming in.

They learn to grab things, and everything goes into their mouths!

They learn to smile and laugh. Stevie
laughs most when he sees Ben make faces.

Before they can walk, babies learn to sit up...crawl...and stand.

Babies can even learn to play games.
Jason had fun playing peek-a-boo with his
little sister, Rachel.

Not all of Rachel's play was fun. Jason was upset when Rachel knocked over his blocks.

Mommy and Daddy try to find ways to keep Jason's things safe from the baby. It helps most times, but not always.

Rachel is still a baby. She doesn't know how to play with Jason's toys. But Rachel loves her big brother and wants to do everything he does.

Your sisters or brothers are different
from you. They may like different things.
And sometimes these differences can make
it hard to get along with each other.

But having different ideas can also make things more interesting.

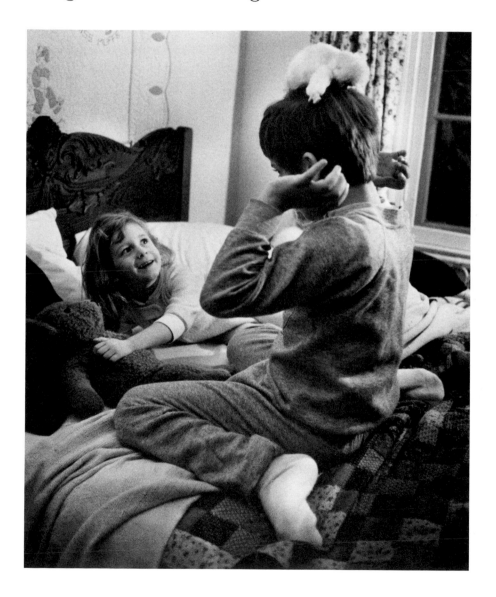

You are different from your sister or
brother. You have your own thoughts, your
own feelings, and your own way of doing
things.

Your parents love you as you are —
the only person like you in the whole world.
They love you because you are special to them.

When his baby sister was born, David was afraid there might not be enough love to go around. But now David knows that love can grow as big as it has to.

Isn't your family like that, too?